insight text guide

Christine Ferrari

Maestro

Peter Goldsworthy

Copyright © Insight Publications 1997

First published in 1997, reprinted 2008 (with revisions), 2011, 2014, 2017, 2018, 2019, 2020, 2023.

Insight Publications Pty Ltd
3/350 Charman Road
Cheltenham VIC 3192
Australia
Tel: +61 3 8571 4950
Fax: +61 3 8571 0257
Email: books@insightpublications.com.au

www.insightpublications.com.au

Copying for educational purposes
The Australian *Copyright Act 1968* (the Act) allows a maximum of one chapter or 10% of this book, whichever is the greater, to be copied by any educational institution for its educational purposes provided that the educational institution (or the body that administers it) has given a remuneration notice to Copyright Agency under the Act.

For details of the Copyright Agency licence for educational institutions contact:

Copyright Agency
Tel: +61 2 9394 7600
Fax: +61 2 9394 7601
www.copyright.com.au

Copying for other purposes
Except as permitted under the Act (for example, any fair dealing for the purposes of study, research, criticism or review) no part of this book may be reproduced, stored in a retrieval system, or transmitted in any form or by any means without prior written permission. All inquiries should be made to the publisher at the address above.

National Library of Australia Cataloguing-in-Publication entry:
Ferrari, Christine, 1947–
Peter Goldsworthy's Maestro / by Christine Ferrari.
9781875882069 (pbk.)
Insight text guide series
Bibliography.
For secondary school age.
Goldsworthy, Peter, 1951– —Criticism and interpretation.
809.3

Cover design: The Modern Art Production Group

Printed in Australia by Ligare Book Printers

contents

CHARACTER MAP

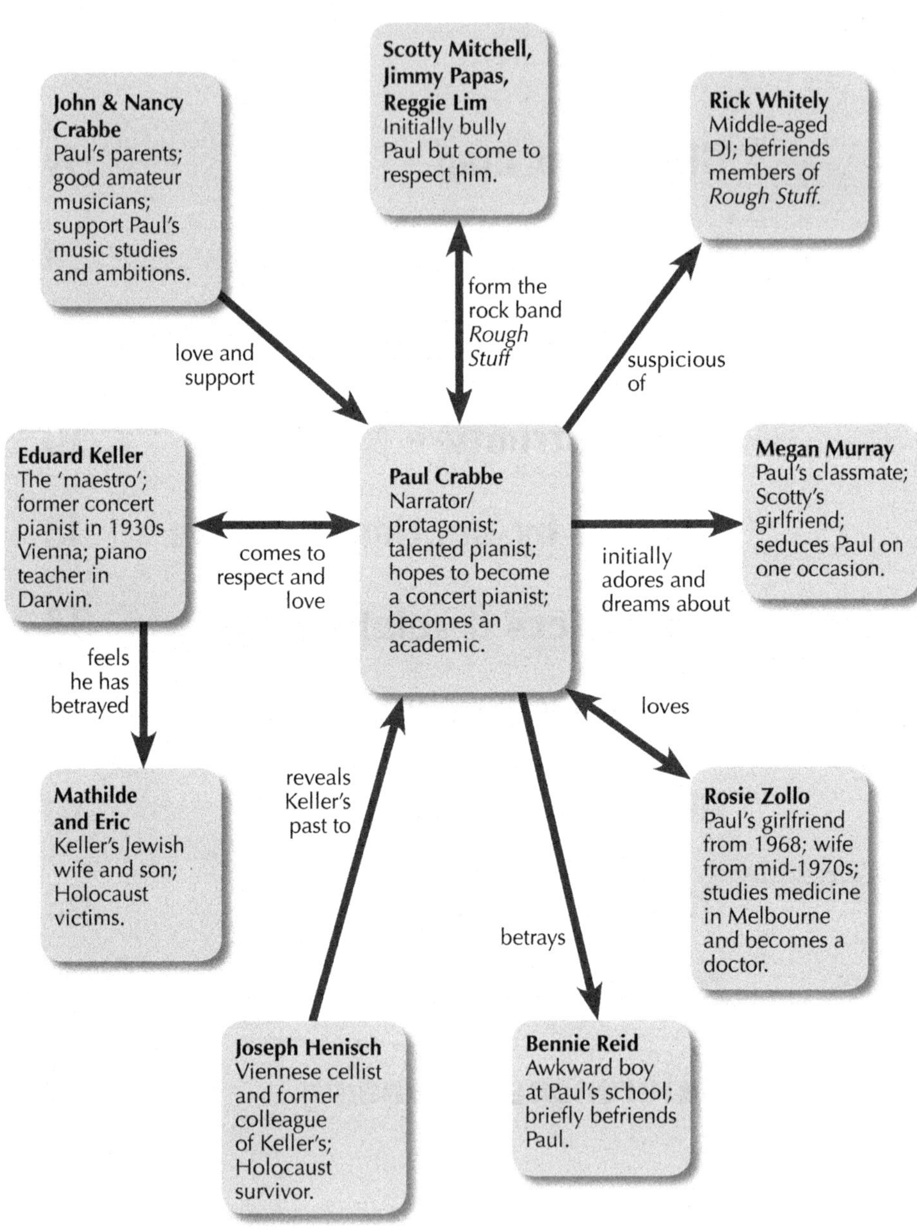

INTRODUCTION

Maestro is a novel about music lessons and life lessons, about growing up and growing old, about coming to terms with past events that defy understanding or easy acceptance. Paul Crabbe, an Australian pianist and academic, looks back over his passage from adolescence to adulthood and attempts to understand the importance of his contradictory relationship with his Austrian-born teacher, Eduard Keller, the maestro of the title. *Maestro* is a first-person narrative whose time scheme covers the years from 1967, when Paul has his first lesson with Keller, to 1977, the year of Keller's death. Paul is imagined by Goldsworthy to be an adult who writes what he calls a 'memoir' recalling his life as a teenager and young man in Darwin, Adelaide, Europe and Melbourne.

The main story is set against the backdrop of the historical events of the Holocaust and the European traditions of classical music focused on Vienna. These factors deepen our appreciation of the plight of Eduard Keller and his cultural isolation in an unsophisticated and materialistic Australia. The contrasting environments of Darwin and Adelaide enrich our understanding of Paul's adolescent experiences and Australian attitudes during the decade of the novel's setting.

BACKGROUND & CONTEXT

Australia and Austria

Austria and Australia? At first glance there is little to suggest a relationship between them, except that one name might be mistaken for another as the epigraph suggests. The epigraph also refers to political scandals in Austria that have attracted worldwide attention – with the implication being that Australia, on the other hand, escapes the attention of the rest of the world.

Darwin and the natural environment

The narrative timeframe of *Maestro* covers ten years of the protagonist's (Paul Crabbe's) life from the age of fifteen in 1967 to twenty-five in 1977. Darwin is the primary setting for *Maestro* because Paul remembers intensely (if with somewhat mixed emotions) the two and a half years he spent there as most relevant to his adult sense of identity.

Darwin's tropical climate with its humidity, and its starkly contrasting dry and wet seasons, seems unreal to Paul when he arrives there after living in a number of country towns. Even retrospectively he conveys his sense of Darwin's exotic strangeness, its 'cartoon world' of 'larger than life' tropical plants and abundant insects (p.11).

Goldsworthy vividly describes the elements of Darwin's natural environment, and draws on these elements in imagery that evokes the relationship between human behaviour and the natural world. One such scene which epitomises the influence of the natural world on humans is when Paul's future is being discussed by his parents and Keller. Paul is impatient because he wants to snatch 'a few minutes at Rosie's after dinner' (p.114). In this lyrical passage he listens to the music of nature:

> Rain was falling outside; the perfumes of the earth folded back on themselves and multiplied. The rich, dank air filled my nostrils; I wanted to be out in the warm rain, pushing through the wet vegetation, physically part of it. The world and I were moulded from the same substances, I knew: we shared the same pollens, scents, sexual triggers, the same cycles of fertility; the same *molecules*. As my father talked wine I closed my eyes and listened to the sounds of the night, to the wet earth smearing itself with greenness: the thickly spread jam of tropical life, a vast croaking, rustling, crawling abundance. (p.114)

This highly sensual passage communicates Paul's instinctual affinity with nature as his sexual relationship with Rosie develops. A distinction between the intellect (the adults are discussing Paul's tertiary education) and the instinctual and emotional (Paul is thinking of Rosie) suggests Paul's psychological immaturity at this stage. As he realises later, he does not take part in the discussion about his further education because he is 'not yet involved in [his] future imaginatively or emotionally; the future was still too far off' (p.114). He feels part of a primitive natural world, and is involved emphatically in the immediate gratification of his desires.

Darwin and Australia's ethnic diversity

Darwin also acts as a microcosm of Australia itself, which only Indigenous people can claim to have occupied for more than two and a half centuries. Australia's multiculturalism is represented in *Maestro*. Bennie Reid is a recent British migrant; Jimmy Papas is of Greek origin; Reggie Lim is part-Chinese, part-Aboriginal; and Scotty Mitchell, like Paul, is a white Australian. As Paul writes, 'the band might have been a statistical paradigm of Darwin's population, a band put together according to the principles of affirmative action and proportional representation' (p.77). Rosie Zollo's name too is foreign, and her mother teaches French. Most importantly, Keller is Austrian.

Key point

Goldsworthy's representation of the mixed backgrounds of the boys at Darwin High School reflects the city's ethnic diversity. The wide acceptance of people from different ethnic backgrounds contrasts with Hitler's obsession with achieving racial purity in 1930s Germany and Austria (see below).

It is worth noting the deliberately muted presence of Aboriginal and Chinese people in Goldsworthy's Darwin – an implicit reminder perhaps that white Australia too has been guilty of genocide, dispossession, and a White Australia policy which restricted Asian immigration based on assumptions of white superiority. The early white explorers, and later British colonists, saw Aboriginal people as lower down the evolutionary ladder than themselves. Chinese people were first brought to Australia as indentured labourers in the 1840s, but their immigration was later restricted by several acts of parliament. By leaving Reggie Lim behind in Darwin when *Rough Stuff* travels to Adelaide, Goldsworthy subtly evokes Australia's shameful history of racism against Aboriginal and Chinese people.

Cyclone Tracy, 1974

The most dramatic Australian historical event in the novel's time scheme is Darwin's devastation by Cyclone Tracy in 1974. In *Maestro*, Paul (who is in Europe) and his parents (who have moved back to Adelaide) are untouched by this experience, although the cyclone destroys the house in which they had lived, and Nancy and John look after Keller until he can return to the Northern Territory. Keller survived the cyclone by sheltering under his *Bösendorfer*:

> wet and shivering and lacerated by flying glass as the roof lifted off the *Swan*, and the walls of his room disintegrated about him, but safe beneath that grand piano. (p.128)

Paul finds this image poetic and strange and searches it for significance. It is only by taking into account Goldsworthy's allusion to rumours of 'mass beach graves containing far more than the official death toll' (p.128), and the fact that Darwin had to be rebuilt after the cyclone, that one can make the necessary jump backwards in time and realise that Keller has lived through yet another catastrophe. While Cyclone Tracy was a relatively minor disaster compared to the Holocaust, and Australia a long way from Europe, the parallel is implicit in the text.

Hitler and the Holocaust

Eduard Keller's family were victims of the Third Reich's program of racial cleansing, where Hitler wanted to eradicate the Jews so that an Aryan master race could rule central Europe. During World War II, the Nazis transported all the Jewish people in the occupied countries of Europe to concentration camps, where around six million Jews were murdered in the gas chambers or died from exhaustion, malnutrition or disease in the labour camps.

Eduard Keller refuses to divulge much about his background in Austria under the rule of Hitler's Third Reich, but what he does say (and the information Paul receives in Vienna from Joseph Henisch) unarguably points to the Holocaust as the turning point in his life.

Keller metaphorically sheltered himself from the German threat to his

Jewish wife and their son by concentrating on his music. He was assured by Adolf Eichmann that 'Jewish members of German families would not be harmed' (p.118). In 1938, Eichmann was in charge of the 'Emigration of Austrian Jews', apparently releasing some people from prison and organising fundraising concerts (p.118). But beneath this sympathetic facade, Eichmann was organising 'the rapid and brutal Jewish emigration policy of the SS in Vienna' (Kershaw 1991, p.149).

Because Paul does not understand the extent of Keller's tragic history until he is a young man, the way in which he comes to learn about Keller's experiences in Europe is crucial. The scene by Keller's bedside as the maestro is dying is one of the most moving in the novel, because the adult Paul now understands the true nature of Keller's background.

Vienna

The cultural and historical contexts behind Keller's musical career and family life help us to understand his personality as well as what lies behind much of his teaching. Paul conveys to his parents the maestro's musical genealogy, its importance underlined by the biblical 'begats' although Paul is using them in a sarcastic manner: '"Beethoven begat Czerny," I recited as best I could. "Czerny begat Liszt. Liszt begat ... Lecherovsky – or someone. And Lecherovsky begat ... Keller"' (pp.19–20).

The names Paul lists – with the exception of Keller – are those of real composers and pianists. Ludwig van Beethoven did teach his friend Austrian Carl Czerny (1791–1857), whose pupils included Hungarian Franz Liszt (1811–1886) and Theodore Leschetizky (1830–1915) who became a concert pianist and opened a school in Vienna where Goldsworthy imagines Herr Keller took lessons. Leschetizky is thought of as the father of modern piano playing techniques. John Crabbe is delighted to discover this lineage, as he has great hopes that his son will be a concert pianist and has unknowingly found him a famous teacher.

Apart from giving his character a realistic European background and impressive musical credentials, Goldsworthy alludes to the city of Vienna as the musical centre it really was. Vienna, the Austrian capital, sometimes called the Land of Music, was the home of numerous famous composers, musicians and conductors including Beethoven, Mozart, Strauss and Mahler. It was also the centre of violent political confrontations during the rise of the Nazi party during the late 1920s and 1930s, a period of world-wide economic depression. Adolf Hitler was also an Austrian, and, as the maestro tells Paul, 'Herr Hitler was an artist ... No one in Vienna enjoyed his art. He left a bitter man. Later he came back – with many friends' (p.116).

'I am Austrian'

Keller maintains his national identity as Austrian when Paul's father suggests that Keller should visit the Barossa Valley because many of its older inhabitants still speak German and 'the culture is very strong':

> 'I am Austrian,' Keller said.
>
> More eye and sign language passed between my parents – pitched at some frequency they seemed to believe beyond his range of hearing.
>
> 'Of course,' my mother said. 'But you *speak* German. It's part of the same culture.'
>
> 'Someone else thought that,' Keller murmured. 'Thirty years ago.' (p.44)

Nancy means well (Austrians do speak the German language), but her conflation of the two countries and their cultures understandably distresses the maestro. Through this dialogue, Goldsworthy appears to remind his readers of the difficulty for many Australians in realising the enormity of events in Europe. But the gaps in the maestro's speeches invite the reader to try to imagine his personal position and thus fill those gaps with reference to the historical context of his character.

Dollfuss and the Anschluss

After the break-up of the Austro-Hungarian Empire in 1918 following the end of World War I, Austria, who fought with Germany against the allies, became a republic. Keller refers to two specific incidents from the period between the wars when he asks Paul: 'You have heard of Dollfuss? Of the Anschluss?' (p.116).

Englebert Dollfuss was the Austrian chancellor in 1933 and 1934. Allied with the Italian fascist dictator, Benito Mussolini, he attempted to keep Austria separate from Germany against the wish of the Third Reich. Dollfuss was assassinated in 1934 after an unsuccessful coup by the Viennese Nazi party.

The idea of a union between Austria and Germany, forbidden by treaties in 1919, gained support in Austria after the collapse of the Habsburg Empire. Hitler pursued the idea once in power, and in 1938, after the forced resignation of the Austrian Chancellor, sent troops into Austria. The union of Germany and Austria – known as the **Anschluss** – was formally proclaimed in March 1938. After World War II, Austria was granted nominal independence from Germany.

Wagner

Because of his personal history, Keller has valid reasons for his dismissive attitude towards the music of Wagner (1813–1883). Wagner's music played a strategic part in the cult of personality which mythologised Hitler, and was promoted by the Nazi Party's propaganda machine. As a twelve-year-old, Hitler was deeply impressed by a performance of Wagner's opera *Lohengrin*. A few years later he attended a performance of another Wagner opera, *Rienzi*, and immediately afterwards a friend listened to Hitler's 'wild talk of leading the German people towards a great future' (Carr 1978, p.139). The overture to *Rienzi* was always played at the beginning of the Nazi party congress, and, as William Carr argues convincingly:

> In Wagner's music Hitler heard 'the rhythms of a bygone world', a pagan world where man lived heroically according to the law of blood, a clean world free of the Jewish 'commercialism' and lust for gold ... where man grappled with the forces of savage nature and lived in a state of mental intoxication (Carr 1978, p.139).

It might be argued that Wagner was simply unfortunate in having his music adored by a dictator whose megalomania and inhumanity has made him infamous, but Wagner was undisguisedly anti-Semitic. Between 1849 and 1851 he wrote an essay entitled 'Judaism in Music'. In *Wagner and his World* (p.55), Charles Osborne describes this essay as a 'notorious anti-Semitic tract' that 'ends by advocating the complete elimination of the Jews from German society and culture'.

Like Wagner, Hitler also drew on nationalistic German mythology and anti-Semitic ideals of racial purity which led to the incarceration and massacre of Jewish people in unprecedented numbers. Wagner's powerful, passionate, beautiful music was utilised in promoting the aims of the Third Reich throughout Hitler's fascist dictatorship. Wagner's music is used extensively, for instance, in Leni Riefenstahl's propaganda film *The Triumph of the Will* (1935) which covers the Nazi party congress at Nuremburg in 1934. How ironic, then, that Goldsworthy provides his character Keller with a wife who is '*the celebrated Jewish contralto and Wagner specialist*' (p.56).

As an opera singer, Mathilde Rosenthal would probably have performed in *Lohengrin* and *Tristan und Isolde*; nevertheless, as a Jewish woman she did not escape deportation to Auschwitz. John Crabbe notes the terrible irony of Mathilde's fate: 'The human angle. *I'm* more interested in the fact that she sang Wagner. I wonder if the poor woman ever sang for the Nazis – they *loved* Wagner' (p.58).

It is therefore not surprising that Keller interrupts the concert in the park when Wagner's Prelude to Act I of *Lohengrin* is played, and that he also avoids the Romantic school to which Liszt (who transcribed Wagner's orchestral music for the piano) and Richard Wagner (who married Liszt's daughter Cosima) belong.

Classical and Romantic music

Romanticism was a nineteenth-century, international movement in the fine arts, literature and music. It promoted revolutionary ideas about form. Its intense fascination with the inner or psychological self, resulting in personal expressions of emotional states and feelings (in keeping with a cult of the individual), is rejected by Keller throughout the novel. So too is the emphasis on the self rather than the collective, on emotion rather than reason, and on the imaginative rather than the real.

During the earlier Classical period in music (1750–1820), when Mozart and Haydn were the most important composers, reason and order took precedence over the emotions. In *Maestro*, during the November Wet when the weather seems to draw Darwin's inhabitants out into the hot, humid world of nature and ballads about 'love, jealousy, murder and jail' spill out into the air, Keller, closeted in his room, emphasises the Classical approach during Paul's lessons as his musical taste narrows:

> Throughout the hot, wet month of November any kind of emotional expression was forbidden, *verboten*: Mozart was played in the manner of Bach, and Bach in the manner of scales, according to strict metronomic markings.
>
> 'Music is a kind of arithmetic,' he told me. (p.50)

Paul wants to return to the Romantics, to 'Liszt and Rachmaninoff, to noise and speed and blurred hands and lyric flashiness' (p.50). The tension in this scene between the controlled rationalism of Classicism and the emotional intensity and rubato of Romanticism is present in many others. Indeed, Keller's over-emphasis on Classicism may adversely affect Paul's playing as he is told – by Henisch, as well as by Keller – that he has a flawless technique but lacks spontaneity and feeling.

The Baroque period and *The Children's Bach*

The first pieces Keller requires Paul to learn, those in *The Children's Bach* (pp.27–8), are from the musical period preceding the Classical period. Music from the Baroque period (roughly 1600–1750) is to some extent like that from the Classical period in being highly structured and following conventional musical forms, with emotions generally being restrained. However, Baroque music can be very ornate and complex, whereas the tendency in the Classical period was towards a more elegant and straightforward style. The most important composers from the Baroque are Bach, Handel and – for keyboard players – Scarlatti.

In fact, few of the simple pieces in *The Children's Bach* were actually composed by Johann Sebastian Bach (1685–1750). A number of them were selected by Bach and included in *Anna Magdalena's Notebook* (1725), which he presented to his second wife. The pieces in *The Children's Bach* were chosen and collected by a teacher at the University of Adelaide, E. Harold Davies, in the 1930s. They are all relatively easy to play and are still widely used as teaching pieces for beginning piano students.

GENRE, STRUCTURE & STYLE

Genre

Maestro is a novel written in the form of a memoir, a collection of reminiscences about a period or a series of events. Paul's memoir includes his rite of passage from childhood through adolescence to maturity, although the most important focus is on the years Paul spent in Darwin during 1967 and 1968 between the ages of fifteen and seventeen. During this period Paul takes music lessons with the maestro who is oddly out of place in the tropical climate. There is an element of mystery, as information about the maestro's past in Austria is only gradually revealed. Interwoven with Paul's preoccupation with the world of classical music and his interest in Keller's past, are incidents from Paul's schooling, his first sexual experiences, and his short-lived career as a member of a rock band.

Paul as first-person narrator

Goldsworthy employs a limited narrative point of view: Paul, as a first-person narrator, cannot know everything about the other characters. We have access to Paul's thoughts and memories, and everything in the novel is described from his point of view.

Key point

The narrator of *Maestro* is some years removed from the experiences he describes. The mature Paul, reflecting on past events, knows much more than the teenage Paul; he can act as an adult 'interpreter' for his youthful experiences.

In order to understand the novel it is necessary to separate the Paul who tells the story from the teenaged Paul. The mature Paul can comment on childhood experiences from an adult perspective. For instance, when Paul completes his final year at university, he sends Keller a tape of his Honours performance. The maestro responds with reams of critical notes which include a veiled invitation to Paul: '*It would be so much easier to play for you than to explain*' (p.125). The young Paul is hurt by Keller's criticisms and decides to spend his two months' vacation with Rosie in Melbourne before leaving for Europe. The older Paul comments: 'An invitation, certainly – but one I chose not to find between the lines at the time', acknowledging that at that time 'most of my love was wasted on myself' (p.125).

The tone of *Maestro*

Maestro is a serious, even tragic novel but it contains heightened moments of humour. Paul sometimes uses self-deprecating humour to describe his younger self (as in the above quotation), and the teenaged Paul, like his father, can make pointedly satiric observations about people and events. Some of Keller's expressions, such as 'Enough of this stool polonaise' (p.112), are amusing and unique, and help to develop his character. Black humour – as in John Crabbe's hospital stories and Keller's newspaper clippings – suggest a less than perfect world, while irony – resulting from the contrast between appearance and reality – is an essential narrative device in the novel.

Style

While the novel draws on a complex mix of styles, realism is an important element. Goldsworthy makes events and characters seem believable by placing his characters in real settings such as Darwin and Adelaide and referring to real historical events such as World War II and the Holocaust, and Cyclone Tracy which devastated Darwin in 1974.

More importantly, given the novel's focus on classical music, are the allusions to real European composers, their musical traditions and compositions, and sometimes, as in Wagner's case, their political affiliations and influence on later historical events. Goldsworthy therefore provides a historical and cultural framework and includes real figures in this fictional text that contribute to its verisimilitude (truth-likeness).

Romanticism

On an imaginative level, Goldsworthy borrows the literary ideas of Romanticism. In Romantic literature, childhood is represented as a glowing period because at that stage the human is instinctually closest to nature – a close relation that is lost as the child matures and becomes socialised. *Maestro* draws on this idea to create a tension between Paul's ideal of what he might have been, and his awareness of human limitations. He longs for the past which was full of opportunity and potential, but which has now disappeared. He learns too late of Keller's suffering and regrets his teenage insensitivity to Keller's needs. This tension is especially evident in Paul's nostalgic reflections on the novel's final page.

Self-reflexive narrative style

While one can define *Maestro* as a realistic novel with Romantic ideas, it also plays with the modernist technique of 'metafiction' where an author draws attention to the story's fictional nature. Again, this creates tension within the novel. Goldsworthy has Paul draw attention to the process of his writing on the opening page as Paul wonders how best to represent the maestro's accent. Elsewhere throughout the text the self-consciousness of Paul's composition is evident:

> No memoir would be possible without this further heading: *The Swan*. So much that is crucial in those years took place in Herr Keller's crowded weatherboard room above the bar of the *Swan*.' (p.17)

This self-reflexive narrative technique is effective on three different levels:

- *Maestro*'s author, Peter Goldsworthy, reminds the reader that any novel (even one which seems 'real') is a fictional work of art which draws upon established literary conventions. The book does not hold a mirror to the world; it is a carefully crafted world on paper.
- Paradoxically, this self-reflexivity or self-consciousness implies that one can trust Paul's sincerity as narrator because he is so careful about shaping his memories for the reader.
- Paul's attention to technique as he writes and his tendency to self-criticism are similar to his approach to playing the piano. Thus, self-reflexivity as a narrative device also assists in constructing Paul's character:

> And so I have wasted the years since Darwin sitting at the piano, pressing keys and hearing only notes emerge, obsessed by technique in a way he [Keller] would never have approved. (p.148)

Structure

The novel is comprised of seven parts: 'Darwin, 1967' with fourteen short sections; 'Intermezzo'; '1968' with eight short sections; 'Adelaide' with six sections; '1974' with two sections; 'Vienna, 1975' with two sections; and '1977' which serves as an epilogue or, in musical language, a coda which is the final part of a musical structure. The close of each short section is marked by a diamond-shaped bullet.

Musical and literary traditions have always been related and you may find it useful to think of *Maestro*'s structure as a series of musical movements with thematic developments, echoes, parallels and variations in tone, mood and style. Motifs (an image, incident or thing) are frequently alluded to throughout the composition and gather symbolic and thematic significance. One such motif is the focus on hands (such as the many references to Keller's missing fifth finger); another is on the idea of wanting to be in the spotlight; and yet another is Paul's use of upper-case letters to signify important people, things or events.

SECTION-BY-SECTION ANALYSIS

The seven main parts of the novel are mostly comprised of short sub-sections. For ease of reference these are set out below as numbered sections with page numbers.

Darwin, 1967

Section one (pp.3–7)

Summary: *Paul has his first lesson with the maestro, Eduard Keller.*

It is 1967 and Paul is fifteen. His mother, Nancy, accompanies him as they move through the crowded, steamy, raucous bar of the *Swan* hotel in Darwin and climb the stairs to Keller's room. Paul's father has arranged the meeting (p.3) in which Keller is to decide whether or not he will accept Paul as a pupil. Nancy feels the heat intensely as the family has only been in Darwin for a month.

Importantly, the older Paul who is writing retrospectively wonders how he should transcribe Keller's accent onto the page: 'A problem: how to capture that accent here?' (p.3). Paul's decision, and the full title he gives to Keller, suggest the development of his respect and empathy over the years: 'from this point in my memoir Keller – Herr Eduard Keller, the maestro – will speak English as well, or as badly, as me' (p.4). This important distinction between the young Paul's impressions and the qualifications made by the more mature Paul who is writing, is introduced in the opening section and becomes crucial to our understanding of the text.

First impressions of Keller

The mature Paul's respect is not so much evident in the description of Keller for first impressions are, as Paul suggests, 'Misleading, of course' (p.4). But the maestro is 'unforgettable' (p.3). He is elderly and an alcoholic – his face has 'a boozer's incandescent glow' (p.3). His alienation from his European birthplace is conveyed by the inappropriateness of his formal, fastidious appearance. His freshly pressed white linen suit, and the stiff collar and tie, seem anachronistic (out of time and place) in this tropical climate. Keller is in his eighties and his chivalry towards Nancy Crabbe contrasts favourably with the drunken wolf whistles she has been subjected to in the bar.

Keller appears curt and cruel as he dismisses Paul's offer to play for him and as he painfully grinds his thumb into Paul's upper arm. To the young Paul, Keller's voice hisses like a snake, and Paul even imagines that Keller clicks his heels together as do Hollywood versions of fascist European characters. Paul is fascinated but fearful and his overall impression is that the man is ridiculous. His pejorative (negative) description of Keller suggests the young Paul's parochialism (narrow-mindedness) and insensitivity: 'He was short: migrant height, European height. Wop height' (p.5).

Keller's hands, in contrast to his ruddy, leather-like complexion, are white and delicate. Paul's attention is drawn to them, and especially to the stump of the right little finger with its gold ring which 'seemed to deliberately flaunt its absence' (p.5). The mystery surrounding the loss of the maestro's little finger is developed throughout the novel. Here, though, Keller is evasive and claims that fifth fingers are a luxury for pianists, although he knows this to be untrue.

Paul's attitude to Keller

During this opening section Paul feels he is undergoing some sort of test and he is deeply resentful. He thinks the maestro's language 'simple and patronising', resenting Keller's comments about his large hands and the maestro's refusal to hear him play. He is embarrassed when Keller catches him staring at the missing finger.

Most importantly of all, Keller almost makes him cry when he presses his thumb into Paul's arm saying: 'Thumb is ... too strong. A rooster, a show-off. Sultan of the harem. He must be kept in place' (p.7). It is possible to read this observation as Keller's initial assessment of Paul who has stared 'boldly' at the maestro and entertained the thought that Keller had 'spruced up especially to meet me' (p.5). The mature Paul adds: 'I was child enough – self-centred enough – to think it likely' (p.5), suggesting a view of himself as a smug and self-satisfied teenager.

Section two (pp.7–11)

Summary: *Paul and his parents discuss the first lesson; they have contrasting responses to their new home in Darwin.*

Paul and his mother return home and attempt to cool down after the suffocating heat of Keller's room, as the pair wait for John Crabbe's return from work. The family discuss the meeting with Keller, which Paul is still 'stewing over' (p.8).

Paul's relationship with his father

We learn that all members of the Crabbe family are musical and that Paul's father has taught his son up until this point. This is important as Paul later thinks of the maestro as a second father. When his parents play a Mozart duet that evening, Paul watches their fifth fingers and thinks, 'I didn't believe a word Keller had said' (p.9). Like his father, Paul is often quick to make judgements. He watches until torrential rain on the iron roof drowns out the music, and John Crabbe irritably pronounces the city the 'arsehole of the earth' as he slams the piano lid.

Adjusting to a new environment

Nancy and John Crabbe are having difficulties in adjusting to the climate and lifestyle of Darwin. Nancy is not yet acclimatised and was horrified at her first sight of their new house. However, her cleaning of the house in preparation for the arrival of furniture suggests her resignation and determination to make a home for the family. Like Keller, Paul's father still wears the formal clothes of a colder environment – his Adelaide uniform of a suit and tie. He makes unfair generalisations about Darwin: 'All the scum in the country has somehow risen to this one town ... All the drifters, the misfits' (p.8). At this stage, John's words and Paul's allusion to Keller as a sadist suggest that Keller may be one of these misfits, but this idea is revised as the novel progresses.

Implied but not stated throughout this section is the strange presence of the Viennese maestro in Darwin. If an Australian family are finding it hard to adjust to a new place, what must the Austrian born Keller have experienced? And why has he come to Darwin?

The landscape and Paul's character

Unlike his parents, Paul has loved Darwin from 'first sight' (p.9). His descriptions of it suggest his sensuousness. The smell of 'hot, steamy perfumes' and 'moist compost air' are combined with an excited sense of adventure (he can't sleep) and an artist's appreciation of the landscape which he recalls vividly (pp.10–11). The closing lines of the section sum up the younger Paul's cartoon-like impressions as he tries to find a metaphor which will adequately convey the unreal sense he has of the place: 'Everything grew larger than life in the steamy hothouse of Darwin, and the people were no exception. Exotic hothouse blooms' (p.11). Because the following section opens with a focus on Keller, Goldsworthy implies that Paul now thinks of Keller as one of these exotic, rare blooms.

Section three (pp.11–13)

Summary: *Paul attends his second or third lesson with Keller.*

Keller is again presented as a paradoxical character. On one hand he speaks simply about the function of the different fingers but on the other,

Paul uses similes to import a sense of violence: 'He sheathed the forefinger in his closed fist as if it were the fleshy blade of a Swiss army knife' (p.11). Paul's mood is extended by his references to the smudged headlines on Keller's white linen sleeves. 'SHOCK, I imagined I could make out from time to time. HORROR. PROBE' (p.12).

Confrontation between Paul and Keller

This section is important in suggesting the initially adversarial relationship between the two. Like John Crabbe, Keller seems rigid in his opinions and is determined to have the upper hand. Paul is reduced to tears as Keller pronounces the boy's edition of Chopin's *Nocturnes* 'unplayable' and drops it in the bin.

Paul is infuriated when Keller grimaces at his offer to play Chopin and when Keller squeezes his wrists and refuses to allow him to play. We get a glimpse of Keller's assessment of Paul's character as the maestro tells his pupil that he is spoilt and too sure of himself, perhaps like the cocky rooster referred to in the first section.

Section four (pp.13–17)

Summary: *Paul reflects on his parents' personalities and relationship.*

The section begins with the mature Paul's meditation on his first memories of Keller. He finds it hard to understand how he moved from these difficult beginnings to come to love and depend upon the maestro.

Father/son relationships

Paul announces that he will not take any more lessons but his father insists he will. When Paul calls Keller a Nazi his father angrily seizes his son and sends him to his room. A pattern is beginning to emerge in these father/son, teacher/pupil confrontations. As an adolescent, Paul resents male authorities who still seem to treat him like a child. Goldsworthy draws attention to this pattern when Paul inaudibly mutters a version of the Lord's Prayer directed sarcastically at his father (p.14).

Link between Paul and Keller's son

As Paul describes his parents' differences, a link with Keller's son Eric is anticipated. Paul sees his parents as opposites: 'When I think of my parents

I see only polarities ... They might have belonged to two different species. Which would make me ... what? Some sort of mule?' (p.15). Later, Keller affectionately refers to his dead son Eric – the child of Austrian and Jewish parents – as 'our mongrel, our *mischling*' (p.118).

Nancy and John

Paul's parents' contrasting attitudes to music reflect their different temperaments and personalities. John thinks of music as 'an interesting kind of clock mechanism' (compare Keller's assertion on page 50 that 'Music is a kind of arithmetic'), whereas Nancy 'allow[s] herself more mistakes' but has 'more fun' (p.16). As a result, Paul is left with an ability to see both sides of a question and therefore to be 'a fence-sitter' (p.17).

Section five (pp.17–18)

Summary: *Paul's lessons continue; he reflects on The Swan and describes his increasing curiosity about Keller's past.*

Paul becomes determined to expose Keller as a Nazi fugitive, but Goldsworthy's focus on Paul's uncertain use of the term, Nazi, as 'a particle of impurity', shows he has little knowledge of its historical meaning. The poster of Vienna with its 'pool-blue river' acts as a contrast to the steamy front bar and suggests that Paul is wrong. Paul also suggests that there is no significant difference between Austria and Germany, a further sign of his ignorance and misplaced self-confidence.

Section six (pp.18–22)

Summary: *The Crabbes discover Keller's former fame as a concert pianist; John becomes more accepting of Darwin.*

John teases Paul about his lessons and the Crabbes are disturbed by Paul's simplistic account of them. But after Paul recounts what the maestro told him about his musical genealogy, his parents are excited to discover that Keller was a famous concert pianist (p.20).

The discovery of Keller's former fame revitalises John, who has previously thought of Darwin in disparaging terms only. He forsakes his suit and tie for the casual clothes more usually worn by Darwin's inhabitants, implying that if Keller lives here the place cannot be that bad. His feeling that he can spiritually transcend the sultry atmosphere and horror stories of the city is suggested by his playing of Liszt and his reverie at Paul's piano lessons.

Section seven (pp.22–7)

Summary: *Paul begins school at Darwin High, is bullied by the local boys and reluctantly befriends Bennie Reid.*

As a skinny, smart new boy, Paul is bullied by Jimmy Papas. The rest of the school follows Jimmy's lead. Paul's only friend is another new boy, Bennie Reid. Both are given names by the other students: 'Big Mouth' and 'Four Eyes'. Paul shows off in maths but otherwise secludes himself in the Music Room. He also alienates Bennie so that his isolation and loneliness are complete.

Why Paul alienates Bennie

As a fellow outsider with an interest in music and in the natural world, Bennie works as a double for Paul just as John Crabbe is a sort of (father-figure) reflection of Keller. Paul turns his back on the person he is like, which suggests he dislikes himself. He compensates for this by showing off at subjects he excels in – like maths – and concentrating on the one thing in which he is superior – music. His isolation in the second-floor Music Room also recalls Keller's isolation in his room at *The Swan*.

Paul's changing attitude towards Keller

Bennie's criticism of Keller as a 'pisspot' motivates Paul to ignore the maestro's wave as the boys ride to school, suggesting that he is not comfortable at being known to associate with this eccentric town character. It also indicates the change in Paul's attitude. Earlier he thought of Keller as a boozer and a Nazi; now he calls him 'my former War Criminal' (p.22). He knows now of Keller's fame and is increasingly curious about him.

Section eight (pp.27–30)

Summary: *Paul finally plays for Keller; John and Nancy hold soirées on Friday evenings.*

Paul plays for the maestro for the first time but feels humiliated when Keller wants him to start with *The Children's Bach*. He complains to his mother that he has been 're-enrolled in kindergarten' (p.27), but his father plays through the pieces that night, telling Nancy of the astonishing 'nuances' that Keller finds in them. The Crabbes have settled into the town's social life, holding musical soirées on Friday nights. Paul's musical skill is appreciated by their friends but this does not compensate for his 'own age group's rejection' (p.29).

Keller is discussed at the soirées, enabling us to learn that he has lived in Darwin for ten or fifteen years. Different theories about Keller are voiced, one of which is that Keller is an Auschwitz survivor (which turns out to be true). It becomes clear that Keller maintains his isolation and does not socialise with anyone in Darwin.

Section nine (pp.30–2)

Summary: *In the Dry, Paul strives for success but never attains perfection.*

During the hot, dry season, Paul finds Keller in the beer garden 'as if the Dry had somehow made him more sociable, more democratic'. However, his bottle of schnapps stands 'high and separate among the amber, lathered beers' (p.30), suggesting his continued difference and isolation from others. That the maestro recalls exactly where Paul's lesson finished the week before suggests the increasing importance of Paul to him. Paul works too hard in an effort to please Keller as perfection seems 'always achingly out of reach' (p.31).

Human limitations

Paul feels that Keller thinks he is not capable of reaching the musical ideals the maestro sets for him. He ignores Keller's advice and constantly seeks to reach a perfect ideal until his hands ache and Keller tells him that 'To search too long for perfection can also paralyse' (p.31).

Key point

Keller identifies only different levels of imperfection and suggests that perfection is an unachievable ideal, and although human beings may strive for it, 'we must know when to move on' (p.31). In other words, we must finally accept our limitations. Ironically, though, Keller cannot forgive himself for his own.

Section ten (pp.32–5)

Summary: *Paul falls in love with Megan Murray, but after asking her for a date he is beaten up by Jimmy Papas.*

In this section Paul's unsatisfying quest for the perfect essence in music is translated into a quest for beauty as he falls in 'love, or lust' (p.32) with Megan Murray. Paul uses self-deprecating humour in this account of his developing sexuality, his dreams of Megan, his approach to her, Papas's warning to 'keep away' and their fist fight after Papas calls him a 'Fucking poofter' (p.34).

Beauty

This section occurs directly after Paul's sense that he has failed to reach musical perfection and it is significant that he thinks of the opening of Megan's mouth as she smiles at him as like 'opening a piano' (p.32). Paul describes Megan as if she is a religious vision, with the sun 'diffracting softly through the edges' of her hair (p.32). The imagined feel of her hair wakes him as he has his first 'wet dream': perhaps a humorous analogy with the effect of the Wet season. The 'glow' of this event lifts Paul beyond the world of thought to 'some high hormonal plateau, feeling manly, invulnerable, immensely content' (p.32).

Masculinity

Paul confuses lust with romantic love, and sex with idealised religious adoration; moreover, it is clear that the object of his love is unworthy of it. During the altercation with Jimmy it becomes evident that masculinity is at stake, as the accusation of homosexuality is the worst insult the boys can think of. This blow to Paul's pride brings him back from his ideal plateau to a bruised reality. His father applauds him for standing up for his rights, which also evokes a stereotypical masculine ideal.

Section eleven (pp.35–9)

Summary: *Paul looks at photographs of Keller's family and learns the names of his wife and son: Mathilde and Eric.*

Paul cannot emulate the notes Keller plays on his grand piano, and attributes this to the upright piano Keller has him play on. He tests his theory when Keller is absent and, as he plays, he looks at the photographs of Keller's family. Only at the end of the lesson, though, does Keller tell him the name of his wife and son.

Keller's past

This is the first direct reference the maestro has made to his past. Even then he makes a distinction between the past and the present by pointing to the sheet music in his room and telling Paul that 'those' are his family (p.38). Nevertheless, the maestro's information further motivates Paul's curiosity, leading him to search the library in Adelaide for information on Keller's background.

Section twelve (pp.39–42)

Summary: *Nancy and John rehearse for* HMS Pinafore.

Sections eleven and twelve are focused on families: Keller's and Paul's. In this section Paul joins his parents in a production of Gilbert and Sullivan's comic opera *HMS Pinafore*. There is tension between Paul and his father as Paul does not want to be hidden in the chorus, but his father says his voice has not broken properly yet. Paul is at the trying stage of being neither adult nor child. On stage Paul's father seems to reveal some repressed 'joyous core' (p.42) and Paul decides that he too wants the spotlight.

In this key event, Paul makes a conscious decision to be famous – 'Centre-stage. Up front' (p.42). He accordingly redoubles his piano practice, practising much more than Keller requires. The image of his father overcoming his habitual pessimism, and allowing a glimpse of the man he might have been, motivates Paul to emulate him.

Work makes free

Keller's 'private joke' at the end of this section carries an ironic deeper meaning. The expression 'work makes free' captures something of Paul's aspirations for success through hard work, but its real significance comes from being the slogan (in German, as *Arbeit macht frei*) at the entrance to a number of the Nazi concentration camps.

Section thirteen (pp.42–6)

Summary: *Paul is successful in his Associate exam, but Keller remains critical and impossible to please.*

Paul's sixteenth birthday and the A+ he received for his music examination are celebrated by the Crabbes, and the maestro comes to dinner for the first time. Keller's presence suggests his pride in Paul's achievement, although he states that the exam is merely a 'technical hurdle' and that Paul is too 'self-satisfied' (p.43).

Keller's past and the Holocaust

Keller reveals several things about his past: he is Austrian, not German, and he refers to the Holocaust and the gas chambers in an understated way. However, when Paul asks about the loss of his finger, Keller avoids revealing the truth by making a joke about no longer being able to clean his ear.

The relationship between Paul and Keller

Paul's performance of one of his exam pieces is pronounced by Keller to be 'technically perfect' but an 'excellent forgery'. Keller compares it to a forged Van Gogh painting he once saw, in which the brush strokes were perfectly copied but which lacked some crucial element of the original. This seems an unnecessarily cruel assessment of Paul's playing, although there might be some truth in it, a sign of how Paul has inadvertently sacrificed spontaneity in order to achieve technical perfection.

It is also possible that Keller is trying to distance himself from Paul because his affection for the boy has placed him in a vulnerable position. In addition, his carefully cultivated facade has been ruffled by the

Crabbes' questions about a past he does not wish to think about.

Keller expresses a significant personal belief when he does not agree with Nancy's view of Vienna as her 'favourite foreign city': beneath its 'Ornamental facades' he sees only hypocrisy (p.45). What is important for Keller is what is underneath those facades: the historical reality, not the architectural illusion.

Section fourteen (pp.46–50)

Summary: *In the Wet, Keller and John Crabbe ponder the strange behaviour of human beings.*

John and Keller become morbid as they brood over the follies of others. They both have a pessimistic view of humanity, and Paul struggles to place his father's 'squalid stories in the same world as the Mozart K. 576 or 332' his father played earlier in the evening (p.47). Keller also dwells on horror stories with his schnapps beside him, hunched over his scrapbooks of newspaper clippings in his shuttered room – the only closed shutters in the town during the Wet. Paul begins to think of the room as a sort of monastery in which Keller can renounce the world.

Beauty in music

In the humidity Keller finds some music unbearable, and Paul is finally reduced to playing scales as 'some kind of ultimate discipline, some perfect control to set against the treacheries of emotion' (p.50). Keller's obsession with control and his change in approach from season to season may explain why Paul's playing lacks spontaneity. Paul argues that 'beauty is what music is *for*' (p.50) and he yearns to play flashy pieces rather than scales. The maestro argues that 'Beauty simplifies' whereas the best music is 'infinitely complex', and he wants to separate music from emotion. He implicitly refers to the Nazis' use of Wagner when he alludes to music as a beautiful vehicle for lies.

Intermezzo (pp.53–9)

Summary: *In the Christmas holidays, the Crabbes stay in Adelaide and Paul discovers the fate of Keller's wife.*

An intermezzo is an interlude or, in musical terms, a short piece of music performed between the acts or scenes of an opera or between other movements of a longer work.

In the university library, Paul is electrified to find that Mathilde Rosenthal died in Auschwitz. Keller's reluctance to discuss his family now makes more sense, as does his bitterness about World War II.

However, Paul's curiosity about Keller's past is dramatically displaced by his curiosity about sex when a couple begin to make love in the library. The 'bristle-furred' hand of the male lover is described distinctly by Paul, implicitly contrasting with Keller's white tapering hands but similar to Jimmy's 'wire-fuzzed' hand described later. For most of the next part of the novel Paul's fantasy world of sex and his desire for fame are priorities as he attempts to bridge the gap between childhood and maturity.

1968

Section one (pp.63–5)

Summary: *Paul meets Rosie; Keller works Paul harder than ever.*

Back at school, Rosie Zollo joins Paul in the Music Room. Although Paul dreams of Megan, Rosie, according to Paul, worships him. Keller works Paul hard as if to contradict the friendship expressed in his sending Paul a valuable Christmas present and when Paul asks leading questions about Vienna, Keller is again bitter about the city, calling it 'The Experimental Laboratory for the End of the World' (p.64). Paul imagines the beauty and excitement of Vienna's musical world, but Keller condemns these dreams and refuses to discuss the city.

Paul and Rosie

Paul is not attracted to Rosie at first because she is too much like him, a similarity that later reinforces their bond. Rosie makes a memorable remark: 'I adore Mozart. It's like … sunlight, don't you think? A dream of sunlight' (p.63). Paul will credit Keller with these words in the epilogue.

Section two (pp.65–7)

Summary: *Keller allows Paul to take one of his scrapbooks home but John Crabbe places it 'out of bounds'.*

In giving Paul the scrapbook Keller wants to 'educate' Paul about the darker side of life. His father, though, sees the clippings as inappropriate. He is not aware that Paul has overheard his own sordid stories. John wants Paul to have his dreams, whereas Keller thinks Paul should be alert to the 'stupidity and squalor' of humanity (p.67).

Section three (pp.67–73)

Summary: *The Crabbes attend an orchestral concert which Keller disrupts; Paul and Rosie begin their relationship.*

The opening is replete with sensual images of tropical fruit which prepare us for Paul's first sexual experience. John Crabbe begins to plant fruit trees and imagines 'recharg[ing]' his 'emotional reservoirs' by buying 'some hilltop dream plantation' (p.67). Contrasting with this fertile imagery is the description of Keller's face as 'a parched landscape'. Because of his past Keller does not allow himself the emotional compensation of dreams.

Rite of passage

Paul's arrogance is evident as, 'feeling carnal, arrogant, invulnerable', he patronises the concert audience (p.70). Keller publicly rebukes him for his sneering rudeness as Paul shows off in front of Rosie. Afterwards Paul and Rosie make love in the Gardens. The adult Paul refers to their younger selves as 'two frustrated loners' (p.73), reinforcing their similarity.

Keller's past

The image of Keller's reaction to Wagner's Act I Prelude from *Lohengrin* stays in Paul's mind and grows clearer as time passes: 'Things I hadn't thought I'd noticed – too immersed in Rosie perhaps – have only surfaced since' (p.71). The older Paul now knows more about history and about Keller's past, and recognises Keller's public outburst as understandable.

Section four (pp.73–5)

Summary: *Paul hears Keller playing Liszt's transcription of Wagner's* Liebestod.

In this section Goldsworthy suggests the connection between emotional states and individual responses to music. Paul, transfixed as he hears Keller playing, identifies the music as perfect; his senses are heightened by his first sexual experience and he hears the music accordingly. Keller, though, staring at the photographs of his wife and child, and knowing more than Paul about Wagner and the Nazis from personal experience, disparages it as trickery. (See Context & Background.)

Section five (pp.75–9)

Summary: *Paul helps Jimmy, Scotty and Reggie to rehearse.*

Jimmy, Scotty and Reggie appropriate the Music Room for their band rehearsals. When they struggle, Paul earns their admiration by playing and then helping them tune their instruments. He offers to join the group for a few weeks and begins instructing them using Keller's words. Paul's sense of himself develops further as he finds a way to control the bullies and to be accepted by his peers for the first time.

Section six (pp.79–82)

Summary: *Megan seduces Paul, but afterwards he returns anxiously to Rosie.*

Megan drives Paul to band practice and seduces him in the bunker of an old fort. Paul's guilt is suggested by the underground setting of the encounter but his masculine sense of power is enhanced by his dreamt-about experience with Megan. He betrays both Scotty (a form of revenge) and Rosie, and Goldsworthy underlines Paul's insensitivity by having Paul visit Rosie immediately after leaving Megan. Sex with Rosie is still furtive and reckless – they are in a caravan outside the Rollos' house – but it is more open and equal than the episode with Megan.

Section seven (pp.82–6)

Summary: *Paul betrays Bennie and cruelly questions Keller about his past.*

Paul is high on happiness and power and feels invulnerable when his parents question the intensity of his relationship with Rosie. His selfishness and arrogance come to the fore, leading to some episodes that cause the narrator Paul to 'squirm' (p.85) in remembering.

In betraying Bennie to Jimmy, Paul may be exacting revenge on Bennie for calling him 'a greasy crawler' (p.84), but it is also an attempt to firm up the approval of the other band members. Paul callously and insistently interrogates Keller, suggesting that he should have left Vienna when the Nazis took over. Keller rightly points out Paul's insensitivity, comparing it to his own.

Section eight (pp.86–92)

Summary: Rough Stuff *wins a local 'Battle of the Sounds' competition.*

Paul receives the easy fame he desires and loves the 'driving rhythms' of the band, the screams of the girls and having his photograph in the local paper. But Paul's confusion is evident in the photograph. Rather than being at the front and in the spotlight, he is 'half-hidden' by the front line. The older Paul can see the irony. While Paul felt Keller's playing of Wagner was perfect because it was music to make love by, he tellingly perceives the sounds *Rough Stuff* makes as 'Music to Shit By' (p.91). His darker side emerges in this section of *Maestro* and the adult narrator shows some contempt for the boy he was.

Adelaide

Section one (pp.93–100)

Summary: *Paul prepares for a piano competition in Adelaide.*

Keller has seen Paul's photograph in the newspaper. Only now does he tell Paul about the piano competition he was invited to enter after his excellent examination result earlier in the year. Keller chooses his moment because he recognises Paul's desire for fame, and perhaps because he is aware of how uncomfortable Paul looked in the photograph.

Keller makes an important point when he tells Paul that he knows how the judges think: 'For them we *pretend* to be athletes. For ourselves, we play music ... we also keep our self-respect' (p.97). This self-respect is missing in Paul's photograph and in Paul's self-assessment. Again, Keller's contradictory attitude towards Paul is evident. He has not told him about the Conservatorium's offer before, but now he begins a series of highly concentrated lessons. His contempt towards Paul is revealed as a facade.

Section two (pp.100–3)

Summary: *Paul stays with his grandparents in Adelaide; Keller prepares him for the competition.*

Paul becomes closer to the maestro than ever before, although his newly found 'Territorian's contempt for Adelaide' suggests his arrogant attitude has not changed. Keller even parodies classical music for Paul in an attempt to lighten the pressure of practice.

Keller is polite to Paul's grandmother, and while he is ironical he remains urbane and charming. He reveals he can do without his schnapps, suggesting that some of his inner needs are being met by the challenge of the music competition. He even pays the highest compliment to his tailor, 'Very fine', another small indicator of the pleasure he is experiencing in Adelaide with his star pupil.

Section three (p.104–7)

Summary: Rough Stuff *arrives and practises in Paul's grandparents' house.*

Paul realises that he is not in charge of the band now Whitely is present. He is disturbed by Reggie's absence. Rick, Jimmy and Scotty reject his re-arrangements of some classical music. When he sees the electric keyboard 'half-hidden' in the lounge room, the maestro murmurs an epigrammatic phrase which leaves Paul puzzled: 'Every fish has its depth' (p.107). He suggests that Paul is enjoying his success in the 'shallows' of popular music, but wonders if Paul is capable of meeting the challenges of classical music.

Section four (pp.107–11)

Summary: Rough Stuff *competes but plays poorly; Paul's lesson goes late into the night.*

Even before the performance, Paul is aware that their ambitions are 'absurd' and their break-up is imminent. In the next lesson, Keller senses Paul's despair at the collapse of his 'squalid, foolish dreams' and attempts to console him by playing some blues (p.109). This music, Keller says, 'simplifies. Prevents thought. Gives easy orders' (p.109). But Paul perceives Keller's pronouncements as 'glib, predictable, even irritating' and his arrogance resurfaces as he announces that they will win next year (p.109).

Paul believes Keller works him late into the night as punishment, but Keller may also genuinely want Paul to achieve success in the Conservatorium competition. This is, we later realise, probably Keller's first public performance since he played for Hitler, suggesting that Paul's assessment of Keller's motives is far too narrow.

In the morning, Paul notices the concentration camp tattoo on Keller's wrist, but Keller still resists talking about what happened to him during the war.

Section five (pp.111–14)

Summary: *Back in Darwin, Paul discusses his future with his parents and Keller.*

Paul, who comes 'a distant third' in the competition (p.112), is back in Darwin during 'the worst dog-days of the Wet' (p.111). Keller comes to dinner with the Crabbe family for the second time in order to discuss Paul's future.

Paul's parents are disappointed although they try not to show it. Keller tells Paul that he should have won the competition, but he discourages Paul from going to a conservatorium for further studies. Paul would like to stay with Keller in order to learn 'the little bits' that make the difference between a good and great pianist, but John believes it is time for his son to move on.

Section six (pp.114–19)

Summary: *Paul visits Keller in* The Swan *for the last time.*

Keller finally relates some of his traumatic past to Paul. He has purchased a new chair and a coffee table so that they can sit opposite each other as equals. He no longer hides behind his music and painfully reveals the political and personal circumstances that led to the deaths of his wife and son. Keller confesses that he 'knew ... these murderers', Eichmann and Hitler, had 'signed their concert programmes' (p.118), had heard of death squads in Poland, and yet felt confident in the assurance that his family would be safe.

Keller cannot forgive himself. He carries both the concentration camp number and his finger stump as marks of his guilt, although how he came to acquire these is not revealed until Paul meets Henisch in Vienna seven years later.

Paul's perspective

Paul is hurt because Keller has told him that Paul's playing lacks that small something which would enable him to become a concert pianist, so his attitude is contradictory. He wants to listen to the maestro because he recognises the importance of his revelation on their final day together as teacher and pupil, but he is also impatient to leave. He can't find the necessary compassion for his teacher because 'The aroused, sexual present overwhelmed the past' (p.117). He loves Keller, but loves Rosie more.

1974

Section one (pp.123–6)

Summary: *Paul studies music in Adelaide.*

Paul studies at the Adelaide Conservatorium where everything Keller taught him hardens 'into dogma'. He describes himself as 'smug, insufferable – and far better at playing the piano than anyone else' (p.123). In his final year of study he sends Keller a tape of his performance and receives a sheaf of critical notes in reply. Keller's remarks contain a barely concealed invitation for Paul to return to Darwin for further lessons.

However, Paul spends Christmas in Melbourne where Rosie is studying medicine, a decision that reflects the strength of the bond between them as well as Paul's desire not to expose himself to Keller's criticisms.

Section two (pp.126–8)

Summary: *In 1974, Paul travels through Europe competing and seeking to establish himself as a concert pianist.*

Paul's parents mortgage their house so that Paul can attempt to make a name for himself overseas. He is still ambitious despite all his 'Honourable Mentions'. Keller sends Paul advice: 'Don't put too much store on winning' (p.127), while Rosie's letters console and encourage him. Ironically, Rosie is keeping a scrapbook of articles about Paul's travels in Europe, which might be seen as another example of (understandable) human folly.

Vienna, 1975

Section one (pp.131–2)

Summary: *Paul teaches piano in Krems, Austria, and seeks information on Keller's past.*

The verbs used in the opening suggest the loneliness and increasing pointlessness of Paul's existence in Europe – Paul is 'beached', 'stranded' and 'railroaded' between 'one competition and the next' (p.131). Goldsworthy implicitly compares Paul's isolation in Europe with Keller's in Darwin. Paul's decision to seek information about Keller indicates, subtly, his realisation that the maestro was right about his talent: his dreams of fame have crumbled.

Section two (pp.132–40)

Summary: *Henisch reveals the crucial details of Keller's past, but refuses to believe that Keller is alive.*

Paul is overwhelmed by the beauty of Vienna – his 'dream city' (p.133). Keller had tried to dampen his enthusiasm by telling him that old Vienna had vanished, but Paul 'believed him even less now than then' (p.133).

Henisch describes the difficulty of leaving Vienna in the 1930s once the Nazis arrived, and the secret Viennese world of locked rooms and hiding places that existed beneath the beautiful city's veneer. Paul's image of Vienna as 'dream city' is undercut by its violent history, and he experiences 'a strange warfare of emotions' on hearing Henisch's account not just of Vienna at that time, but of Keller's musical tastes and performances. Keller's love of the Romantics with their 'big strong sound' does not tally with Paul's experience of the maestro's Classical taste in music, and with Keller's dismissal of the Romantics as insincere. Paul realises that the man he knows is 'not the same man, in a sense' (p.140).

1977 (pp.143–9)

Summary: *Paul returns to Darwin and visits Keller in hospital; on Keller's death, Paul reflects on his teenage years.*

Paul has changed markedly. He is subdued, resigned and sadly even thinks he is approaching middle age at twenty-five. His dreams of fame have disappeared and he is now unhappy to be teaching music.

Paul addresses Keller respectfully in German as Maestro, and means it for the first time. His care for the maestro, who is often unconscious, shows his compassion. Yet he attributes to Keller something Rosie and not Keller had said: 'Mozart shines like the sun' (p.144). Paul would like to think of Keller in this pleasant way, but this is not the tormented man who had lived for years in a shuttered hotel room in Darwin. Perhaps Paul is imagining the idealistic man Keller had once been; or perhaps Paul's own idealism and nostalgia are colouring his memories.

Loss and nostalgia

Paul's grief is evoked in his need to tell someone that 'a Great Man had died' (p.146). Even the Darwin he knew in his childhood has vanished. Alone in his hotel room, he faces himself wholly for the first time. While Keller was alive, the promise of 'a last assault on the world of music' was a possibility; now Paul believes he has 'wasted the years since Darwin' (p.148). Despite his despair, the Romantic in Paul surfaces as he enjoys the sunset. He has the emotional balance in his character which Keller had tried to repress.

The novel's ending threatens to tip into sentimentality as Paul becomes nostalgic for his childhood, although the reader who has shared this world may see little of the ideal about it. But the images which flash into Paul's mind are positive ones of his mother with light behind her, his father holding his home-grown rambutan, and Keller 'sitting in a shaft of sunlight' (p.149). The final lines suggest Paul forgives himself for everything.

CHARACTERS & RELATIONSHIPS

Paul Crabbe

Key quotes

'Skinny, unathletic, irredeemably smug ...' (p.25)
'Only now can I recognise the scene for what it was: a confessional, a privilege that I, through selfishness and sensual addiction, failed to accept.' (p.117)
'Now I was faced with myself for the first time: Paul Crabbe, greying, dissatisfied, fast approaching mid-life ...' (p.148)

At fifteen Paul Crabbe is a gifted pianist whose world is filled with music. Because of his father's work, the family has moved frequently, producing amateur productions of comic opera wherever they live. His parents play the piano nightly, and as a baby in a bassinette Paul lay under the piano while his mother rehearsed Gilbert and Sullivan. Music is the glue in Paul's life. Paul is a shy loner, possibly – although it is never stated explicitly in the text – because he has had to move from school to school. He is also an only child.

Paul's arrogance has perhaps developed as a protective shield – when he begins school at Darwin High, for instance, he is ostracised (excluded) by a group of bullies who call him 'Big Mouth' (p.23). He is intelligent and smug, slamming his 'pen loudly onto my desk at the end of each maths problem to let the plodders know I had finished' (p.25). He rides his bicycle to school rather than catch the bus and takes refuge in the school's Music Room during every lunch hour. Goldsworthy evokes the boy's sense of isolation when he describes the school's location from Paul's point of view: 'The High School, isolated on its headland like some kind of quarantine station, or detention centre, seemed miles from the nearest human habitation' (p.24).

Paul's only friend is Bennie Reid who is also new to the school and Australia and whose nickname is 'Four Eyes' (p.23). Paul shuns any association with Bennie at school, but at weekends accompanies him through the bush as Bennie collects butterflies, which Paul fails to mount and label as perfectly as his friend. Paul breaks off the friendship, possibly because he sees himself in Bennie whom he describes cruelly as 'whining in the door of the Music Room' (p.26).

Paul and Keller

Paul's relationship with Keller is therefore very important to him because, although Paul might be at the bottom of the school hierarchy, he is, as his father tells him, a very talented musician. The maestro sees his arrogance immediately (perhaps he sees something of himself or his son in Paul) and maintains a facade of polite contempt. He re-teaches correct fingering techniques to Paul, who is humiliated. John teases Paul after each lesson: 'Played anything yet?', and Paul convinces himself that the maestro is a war criminal in exile.

As an isolated only child, Paul enjoys the appreciation his parents' friends show for his musical talent, but at his piano lessons he does not receive such praise. Even when Paul does extremely well in his Associate exam, Keller typically withholds any real praise, gruffly telling the Crabbes that their son is 'too given to self-satisfaction' (p.43). Keller's tone seems rude, even cruel, but the older Paul suggests he might be telling the truth.

The young Paul's feelings are more ambivalent (uncertain). He secretly names Keller 'Adolf', but also practises more than Keller requires him to (p.42). Paul's choice of a European snowy Christmas card which he hopes 'might bring a little coolness into Keller's steamy room' (p.54) suggests his affection for Keller. If Keller is missing Paul, as his gift of precious sheet music suggests, then Paul, who spends much of his time in the library seeking information about the maestro, is also implicitly missing his teacher.

Other relationships and growing up

Paul's world widens as he becomes sexually experienced and becomes a member of *Rough Stuff*. Both developments are ironically connected with different types of music. He looks forward to his 'First Time' after watching the couple in the library while 'an assortment of musicology texts' comically fall down on him (p.57). Paul and Rosie make love after the outdoor concert. He is introduced to rock and roll with the band. Keller (like Paul's schoolwork and family) now takes second place to Rosie and the band, although the music lessons provide continuity in Paul's life. For the first time, Paul does not take part in the yearly Gilbert and Sullivan production.

During these months (and most of 1968, the third part of the novel) Paul feels 'high, happy, invulnerable' (p.82); 'carnal, arrogant, invulnerable' (p.70). Joining *Rough Stuff* allows Paul to rebel against the disciplined complexity of the maestro's lessons, become the decision maker, and find protection in making allies of his former bullies. Even the loss of the Adelaide Battle of the Sounds and the disappointment of third place in the piano competition do not seem to dampen his high spirits or youthful impetuosity.

Facing the truth

In Europe, Paul is forced to face the truth about his talent. On his return to Australia he marries Rosie and later sits at the maestro's bedside as the elderly man dies. The older Paul is a discontented man responsibly working at employment he hates but happy within his own family circle. The scenes in the hospice show Paul's thoughtfulness and love for the maestro, as well as the overwhelming sense of loss he feels when Keller dies without Paul ever explaining that he understands why the maestro felt he had to hide his emotions. It is this mature, rational and saddened Paul who writes the book as a tribute to the maestro, forgives himself for the insensitivities of his childhood, and reflects nostalgically on his loss.

Eduard Keller

Key quotes

'... the red glow of his face – a boozer's incandescent glow. The pitted, sun-coarsened skin – a cheap, ruined leather. And the eyes: an old man's moist, wobbling jellies.' (p.3)
'I remember the hands: those dainty, faintly ridiculous hands.' (p.5)
'Contempt and self-hatred fuelled the singing of the voice, and all the while the hands played, autonomously, with an abandon and rapture beyond anything I had ever heard.' (p.73)

Eccentric, forbidding, withdrawn, wise, arrogant and tragic, the character of Eduard Keller looms over this novel. As the title suggests, he is the central, dominating figure; the development of his over-critical yet increasingly affectionate relationship with Paul generates the narrative drive as the story of Paul's rite of passage runs parallel with the revelations about Keller's past.

Keller's appearance

Keller is the only character whose appearance Goldsworthy describes in full detail. We have a vague idea of how Paul and his family look – thin, ungainly, dark or fair – and Paul provides some insight into his parents' thoughts and of course his own as narrator; but we know exactly how Keller looks.

We know the contours of his elderly face with its glowing and coarse complexion, its moist eyes. He dresses impeccably, if absurdly, in a clean and pressed white linen suit with a stiff collar and tie. We know exactly how his hands look even down to the missing finger on whose stump he wears a gold ring. He wears a pince-nez, has perfect manners although he can be devastatingly sarcastic and dismissive, and he is too fond of alcohol.

Key point

Keller has the appearance of an eccentric stage character and this is an important clue to his character, because he is playing a part. The maestro has placed a solid wall between the passionate man he used to be and the gruff, disgruntled, detached and intensely private man he now appears to be.

Keller's past

Due to the terrible events in his past, Keller has disassociated himself from his birthplace. He chooses a country whose name sounds like his own but is on the opposite side of the world. Like Paul, we are only given glimpses of the man the maestro was before he ensured his transportation to a concentration camp by sewing on the yellow star Jews were ordered to wear by the Nazis. Although Keller is not Jewish, he took this action after his Jewish wife, Mathilde, and son Eric were deported. This may have been a form of self-punishment or penance because he blamed himself for their deaths.

As readers, we gradually piece together Keller's story. He had the opportunity to leave Vienna after the Anschluss. His wife, an opera singer, suddenly found 'there was no future for her', but Keller optimistically believed 'The evil would pass' and that no one 'would harm the wife of Eduard Keller' (p.117). When he is commanded to play for Hitler he does so, believing that being so highly visible might ensure his family's safety (p.136). His self-contempt lies beneath the facade of his eccentric, buttoned-up appearance. Paul witnesses an expression of this when he finds Keller singing as he plays Wagner's *Liebestod* (p.73).

Despite the extreme circumstances, Keller cannot forgive himself. He attempts to alienate himself from all feelings and carries a physical sign of both the love he had for his family, and his present sense of impotency, in the stump of the little finger of his right hand on which he wears a wedding ring. We have a hint of what happened to this finger when he tells Paul his finger offended him but he 'could not – how do you say it – finish the job' (p.119). The implication is that he intended to cut off all his fingers, and indeed Henisch recalls that in the concentration camp, Keller 'told me that if he ever felt the desire to play again he would hack off his fingers, one by one' (p.138). When Paul plays in the piano competition in Adelaide, Keller accompanies him and thus gives a public performance for the first time since his family's death. He does this for Paul, not himself.

Keller's musical preferences

The tension between Keller and Paul is often represented in the sort of music they favour. Paul is swept away by Liszt and Wagner, yet Keller denounces their music as trickery. He teaches Paul Classical composers like Beethoven and Mozart, or selected Romantics like Chopin and Brahms. Keller emphasises the head rather than the heart. This may affect Paul's piano playing because he becomes more obsessed with the technical aspects of his music and channels his emotional passions into love-making. Yet in Vienna, Keller loved the Romantics and was 'a passionate virtuoso' (p.139).

When Paul visits Vienna and speaks to the cellist Joseph Henisch, Paul announces that Keller 'loves Bach and Mozart. And the later Beethoven. He hates the Romantics. Empty rhetoric, he calls it' (p.138). Henisch replies that 'Eduard Keller would never play Mozart if he could play Liszt, or Rachmaninoff. He liked to entertain. He liked a big, strong sound' (p.138). Indeed, Henisch gives Paul the last recording Keller made, containing Liszt's *Hungarian Rhapsody No. 3* and Liszt's piano transcription of the *Liebestod* from Wagner's opera *Tristan und Isolde* (p.139). Yet Paul saw Keller's disturbed, disruptive reaction to Wagner's *Lohengrin* in Darwin (pp.71–2), and heard his contemptuous playing of the *Liebestod*:

> I knew the piece well; Wagner again. My father often played orchestral excepts from *Tristan* on his gramophone. But I had never heard it played quite like this; a piano transcription, accompanied by snorts of contemptuous laughter, and phrases of angry, broken singing. (p.73)

In this scene Goldsworthy shows us the split between the emotional power of Wagner's music which Keller plays and his passionate need to distance himself from it. We receive a glimpse of why Keller was a famous musician. He plays from memory, his hands moving 'autonomously, with an abandon and rapture beyond anything [Paul has] ever heard' (p.73). However, Keller despises himself for it because of all Wagner's music has come to mean for him.

After Paul plays Beethoven's *Arietta* for Henisch, the cellist says he knows they are not talking about the same Eduard Keller. Paul's technically flawless playing lacks '*rubato*', the flexibility of tempo, 'the rapture and abandon' which characterised the playing of Keller's pupils and of Keller himself (p.139). Paul knows it is the same man, but he also realises that the Eduard Keller who played with passion and *rubato* did die symbolically after his wife and son died in the Holocaust.

John Crabbe

Key quote

'I suspected I was glimpsing some part of him that had been long repressed: some frivolous, joyous core that hardship, childhood tragedy and the War had buried inside him for too long.' (p.42)

Paul's father is a hard-working doctor whose real love is music. As Paul says, 'Medicine was his job, music his life' or in John's own words: 'medicine was his wife, music his mistress' (p.39). Paul refers to him as 'stoic' in contrast to the relatively 'emotional' Nancy (p.15). John's work can exasperate and astound him as his stories of the more bizarre cases suggest (pp.47–8), but he is 'a connoisseur of the human comedy' (p.47) and a master of irony: 'Farmers are paid not to grow crops. We pay Keller to stop Paul making music. Possibly it will increase the value of the product' (p.19). At home, music, particularly that of Mozart, acts as a sort of tranquilliser for him (pp.9, 49). It also brings the family together.

Under pressure of work, and his initial sense of guilt because he believes he has dragged his family to 'the arsehole of the world', John can become irritable, even morbidly brooding (p.9). He can be authoritarian when he gives Paul orders and he will not tolerate Paul's uninformed judgements of the maestro (pp.8, 13). He can also be insensitive in humiliating his son, even when he is simply stating the truth, as he does when casting Paul in the chorus of *HMS Pinafore* (p.41). John's love for his son is strong, but is not always clearly demonstrated to him – Paul describes his father kissing him goodnight when he believes Paul is asleep (p.14).

Although we are not given a detailed account of John's youth, Nancy suggests the difficulty of his early life when she explains to Paul that John did not have the same opportunities as his son (p.14). His wish to pursue a musical career was presumably given second place to the need to earn a living, and later to the demands of war service. The Christmas gifts of valuable sheet music he gives to his son when Paul is very young and expecting toys, suggests John had missed the small childhood joys that most people take for granted. And in many ways, his thwarted musical ambitions are realised through Paul.

The opportunity of producing and appearing in amateur productions of Gilbert and Sullivan comic operas delights him. The stage becomes a place where he can express emotions through music and song. To Paul, the onstage man appears quite different to the father he knows:

> strutting the stage in a parody uniform and a kilogram of jingling medals, singing absurd songs at breakneck speed, bathing himself in the laughter and applause. At these times – and afterwards, kite-high on excitement – he bore no resemblance remotely to anyone I knew. (p.42)

John Crabbe is an intelligent, well-read man who is extremely knowledgeable about music and its history. He understands at once the terrible irony of the maestro's life in Europe because World War II disrupted his own life (p.14) and his attitude towards the maestro is often used to guide our own response to Keller. Indeed, John can be seen as a scaled-down, more emotional version of Eduard Keller. His character therefore performs important functions in a text in which there are so many silences.

After he becomes aware of Keller's musical genealogy he attends Paul's lessons and listens intently to everything the maestro says. This knowledge is the catalyst for his change in attitude towards Darwin itself. Previously he placed himself in a superior position because he came from the south and was overly dramatic in his pronouncement: 'All the scum in this country has somehow risen to this one town' (p.8). The new knowledge of Keller's background helps him to transcend (rise above) his first impressions and Goldsworthy provides a humorously ironic note as he has John play Liszt's *Transcendental Studies* (p.21). Paul notes 'from that morning his mood seemed altered, lifted into some zone of clearer, fresher mental weather' (p.21). From this point John attempts to fit into life in the Northern Territory, rather than remaining aloof and judgemental about it.

Nancy Crabbe

Key quote

> 'My mother was sloppier [than John], allowing herself more mistakes, but in the end she had more fun.' (p.16)

From a feminist point of view, Nancy Crabbe could be seen as a stereotypical domestic character. The family is a traditional nuclear one with the father as breadwinner. Nancy has lived in numerous small towns because John's career makes this necessary. We get a hint of the difficulties of new adjustments when Paul sees her crying in despair when they first arrive in Darwin, but she is practical and soon adjusts. The former librarian has chosen to stay at home although she prefers playing piano to housework (p.16). Nancy acts as a mediator between her husband and son when necessary and Paul sees her as the complete opposite of John, but although there is tension in the relationship their disagreements are often light-hearted.

That Nancy is more demonstrative than John is suggested when she speaks with Paul after his father has sent him to his room. Paul leans back against her body as she talks to him (p.14). From Paul's limited point of view his parents' marriage is happy, bound together by music and 'the sweet, sticky glue of sex perhaps' (p.16). Paul does not mention the other thing which implicitly binds them together – their son and their hopes for his future. They love showing off Paul's musical skills to their social group, and they discuss his future at length.

Nancy also makes the props for the amateur performances and Paul remembers that the 'exquisite stage props were often fashioned even more carefully than the objects they represented: Art not so much imitating as improving upon Life' (p.40). Nancy can also be thought of as improving on the itinerant style of life she has to lead because of her husband's work. She makes the best of her family's circumstances. Is Paul also improvising and improving on life on the final page of *Maestro*?

As Paul grows older, Nancy's emotional support becomes less important to him. When the family visit Adelaide for Christmas, Nancy shows Paul how to use the university library. When they work closely in their search for information about the maestro, they have a close and affectionate relationship. During the following year after Paul and his school friends have formed *Rough Stuff,* Nancy questions the wisdom of the band's trip to Adelaide and protests that she does not know the other boys. Paul responds, 'They're my *friends,* Mother'. The older Paul's reflection on this episode suggests the boy's desire for independence:

> Mother. Was this the first time I had used the word in that way – keeping her at a distance, as if with a verbal barge pole. Certainly somewhere in that year she had made the transition from Mum to Mother: the journey of nuances. (p.96)

This reflection is one of the markers of Paul's rite of passage from childhood to young adulthood. Goldsworthy may be implying that Paul's successful relationship with Rosie is a result of his earlier secure, close relationship with his mother which is no longer necessary.

In the opening section, Nancy Crabbe's character functions to suggest that Paul's assessment of Keller is distorted. Throughout most of the text, however, her role is only important in relation to her son and husband and her character is mainly used to explicate (reveal) theirs.

Rosie Zollo

Key quote

> 'Those nights of deepest, first-discovered joy in Darwin had never left us; each term's separation only magnified our memory, and desire.' (p.125)

Rosie is Paul's first and only girlfriend: the couple later marry and have a child. She is a warm, generous and sensual young woman who is Paul's equal intellectually but not musically. In some ways she is like Paul's mother in that she is totally supportive and has a healing influence when Paul is depressed. She too improves upon life. She writes weekly letters to Paul when he is in Europe, in which she 'seemed always able to tell me exactly what I wanted to hear' (p.128). Rosie has her own career as a doctor but her main role in this novel is as Paul's loyal lover and nurturer. Once again the world of *Maestro* is male-centred: its female characters are important only in relation to the male ones.

Megan Murray

In direct contrast to Nancy and Rosie, who are nurturing stereotypes, Megan is a vamp (another stereotype) whose beauty nevertheless appears angelic to Paul as he watches her in class. Megan has smooth, downy fair skin, 'a wide keyboard of white, perfect teeth' and a 'thick cumulus of pale hair' (p.32). To Paul she is 'a haloed vision' (p.32). When Paul tells her he dreamt about her she is patronising, telling Paul: 'I already have a man' (p.33). Megan is vain, careless and shallow, humiliating Paul, passing his confession on to the bullies and later seducing him.

Bennie Reid

Bennie is the boy Paul does not want to be – frail (he is always breaking limbs) but tubby, effeminate, an inept musician and apparently a natural victim – a 'nerd' in colloquial language. Paul and Bennie are doubles. Bennie is a comic character but he is also patient and skilled in mounting and classifying the butterflies he collects. He, like Paul, is a lover of beauty. Paul always thinks of him as middle-aged and balding, so perhaps he is wiser than Paul. Note that Paul *follows* Bennie when they go out to collect butterflies (p.25).

In their second year at Darwin High the boys show the differences in their personalities by their attitude to the bullies. By joining *Rough Stuff*, Paul finds a non-confrontational way of achieving his revenge and 'permanent protection in the schoolyard' (p.79). But Bennie courageously faces up to Jimmy and has the last word even though he is battered (p.84). He anticipates Paul's betrayal and angrily slams the door in his former friend's face (p.85). Paul looks weak in comparison. Although everyone is surprised when Bennie is accepted at the Naval Officer's Training School his potential for leadership and courage is evident, and his choice of profession offers him a stronger masculine position than he has experienced at school.

Jimmy Papas

The child of over-indulgent wealthy parents, Jimmy is king of the schoolyard. He is 'short, thickset and wire-haired' and wears a permanent sneer (p.33). Convinced of his own masculine strength he bullies anybody he perceives as different:

> All over Darwin the slightly built, the bespectacled, the swots and the Sunday School students would lie in their beds at night, planning revenge on short, squat Jimmy Papas. (p.76)

Paul makes a distinction between the bullying of Scotty and Jimmy. Whereas Scotty needs to be provoked into violence, Jimmy's cruelty does not have an emotional trigger; it is 'arbitrarily dispensed, nothing more than a way of filling in time, a form of impromptu entertainment' (p.76). Paul sees Jimmy as a 'wild animal' (p.79). Jimmy's panel van with its sticker: 'DON'T LAUGH – YOUR DAUGHTER MAY BE IN HERE' makes him even more the hero leader as he leaves rubber on the roads and swaggers around school (p.83). But he doesn't have a girlfriend. Jimmy becomes Whitely's henchman and the DJ puts his 'mark' on Jimmy by convincing him to have a tattoo.

Scotty Mitchell

Scotty is one of Jimmy's underlings, a boxing champion, Megan's boyfriend and lead guitarist in the band. According to Paul, Scotty – in contrast to Jimmy – at least seems to believe in something:

> Scotty believed in Just Causes – however unjust they appeared to others. Not so much Protecting the Weak, for instance, as Sticking Up For A Mate. If he beat up someone half his size, it was not for pleasure but reluctantly, necessarily, to teach his victim a lesson. (p.77)

Unlike Jimmy, Scotty at least senses Whitely's shady interest in young boys (p.89). But still he cultivates his friendship because of his Chuck Berry tapes and his contacts with the rock music world. Scotty tells Paul to 'lay off' Whitely because 'He's a good mate' (p.106). Still, although Scotty later feels guilty about leaving Reggie behind, his version of mateship seems highly selective. He is impressionable and under Whitely's squalid influence.

Reggie Lim

Reggie is a member of Jimmy's group perhaps because of the fierce look of his face with its acne scars. But he is 'a follower, not a leader' (p.77). He simply echoes the words of the others, although Paul calls him 'an occasional comedian' (p.87). As the drummer of *Rough Stuff* he is at least the centre of attraction for a crowd of younger, 'smaller Reggies' (p.91). Reggie is important as a representative of minority groups in *Maestro*.

Rick Whitely

Like Jimmy Papas, Whitely is represented as an unlikable, egocentric character. He is dishonest and Goldsworthy invents a shadowy past for him. Whitely is clearly attracted to Jimmy and acts inappropriately with the boys, stripping in front of them, fixing the band competition, fostering their under-age drinking and taking them to an all-male club. He has the trappings of a rock guru – the permed afro hairstyle, the wide Zapata moustache – but he is brutish and narrow-minded and has been sacked from various radio stations.

To the boys he represents rebellion and their chance for fame and money because he is judging the Battle of the Sounds contest in Darwin. He uses his power over them in a questionable way. Whitely convinces the boys to leave Reggie behind – this is ironic, because although he appropriates black culture in his afro hairstyle, and although rock and roll has its roots in African-American music, he rejects Reggie, who is a person of colour. Because both Whitely and Keller act as mentors in Adelaide during the two competitions, Goldsworthy implies that we should compare the backgrounds and behaviour of these two very different characters.

Mrs Wallace

Paul's maternal grandmother is another nurturing woman. Her gently comical character comes through in her dialogue with the maestro (p.100). Her attempts at small talk with Keller (who addresses her as 'dear lady') are funny and she fusses over him. The maestro's responses are often ironic but he is always polite, in contrast to Whitely who invites himself and the band into her house, and rudely cuts off her response.

Josef Henisch

The cellist Joseph Henisch is the only character who knew Keller in Vienna. What he has to say is crucial for an understanding of the maestro's character: it fills in the 'blanks' in the story of Keller's experiences under Nazi rule, and explains why so many people (including Henisch) think that Keller died during the war. Henisch also sheds light on Keller's pre-war musical tastes, which Paul (and the reader) would otherwise have no knowledge of.

THEMES, IDEAS & VALUES

Rite of passage

A major theme of the novel is Paul's transition from adolescence to adulthood – his 'rite of passage'. Paul feels he has to prove his manhood and establish his masculinity with his peers; at the same time, he is involved in a complex relationship with Keller as he attempts to develop into a world-class concert pianist in adulthood. He has to overcome his youthful smugness, arrogance and lack of self-knowledge. His passage to adulthood involves the loss of his dreams and learning to at first recognise, and then to forgive himself for, his youthful insensitivity.

Loneliness

Paul and the maestro are loners. Keller has chosen exile from his native land and stays in his shuttered room. Similarly, Paul avoids contact with his peers and practises in the Music Room every school lunch hour. Music offers some consolation to both the maestro and Paul, and they develop a guardedly affectionate relationship because of it.

In *Rough Stuff*, Paul, like the other boys, dreams of fame and fortune although he is at first motivated by 'private revenge' (p.79). For the first time he mixes with those of his own age at weekends, practising with the band, going to the drive-in or swimming. But joining the group leads Paul to turn his back on Bennie and betray Rosie with Megan. Keller comes out of his own isolation to accompany Paul in Adelaide.

Looking back, Paul's most vivid memories are not of the band but of Keller: 'the ancient brick-faced Viennese virtuoso in his white suit, belting out twelve bars of fast blues' (p.109). In Europe, Paul experiences desolation and loneliness as he teaches music in Krems between competitions. His position in a lonely room, secluded linguistically from others, is similar to that of the maestro in Darwin. He makes the decision to 'piece together the various fragments of [Keller's] life, beginning with what he'd told me in our last conversation together' (p.131).

Human limitations

Keller's wish to communicate a sense of human limitation to Paul comes from his affection for the boy and is the result of his loss and consequent sense of self-contempt.

Paul's dream of becoming a virtuoso eludes him as Keller predicts. Keller tells Paul that he is his 'best student, yes. One in a thousand. But a concert pianist is one in a million' (p.113). The maestro is giving Paul an honest assessment so that he can avoid further disappointments.

Implicit in his attempt to make Paul face reality is Keller's belief that his own life has been wasted because he, like Paul, had been arrogant and insensitive. In spite of the annexation of Austria, his wife being ignored by the musical world and rumours of deportation, Keller felt optimistic. He tells Paul that in one's own home 'it is more difficult to see evil' (p.118). As a famous pianist he believed that maintaining high visibility by playing for Hitler would keep his wife and son safe. But he misjudged the extent of the evil and constantly reminds himself of the failures of the human race by keeping his 'textbook' of newspaper cuttings. He attempts to repress all emotions and maintain a rational view of the world because he now sees his former feelings of invulnerability and optimism as criminal in the circumstances.

John Crabbe is also pessimistic about humanity. Like Keller he broods over the bizarre things he hears at the hospital, maintaining a pessimistic view of a 'bleak human landscape located somewhere between Tragedy and Dumb Stupidity' (p.65). But unlike Keller, he does not think the scrapbooks are suitable material for his son. John dreams of owning a small hilltop farm and has hopes for his son. Unlike Keller, he has the support of family life. He is more balanced in his assessment of humanity and recognises the place of optimism and dreams in his son's life. His claim that Paul needs to find out for himself whether he is good enough to be a concert pianist sounds like common sense. Perhaps working towards a goal, rather than the achievement of it, is valuable in itself. Paul's final thoughts in *Maestro* about 'a foolish, innocent world, a world of delusion and feeling and ridiculous dreams' (p.149) on which he can look back with love may substantiate this idea.

The deceptiveness of beauty

The maestro distrusts the beautiful external appearance of Vienna and the beautiful music to which lies were set during the war. He has his libretto of ugly poetry to set against the fascination of beauty. The beautiful can become intoxicating so that one loses sight of reality. The young Paul takes beauty at face value, not having learned to see beyond surface appearances. When he is seduced by Megan who has fuelled his sexual fantasies, he realises that the sum of Megan's beauty is 'somehow less than its parts' (p.81). The theme of beauty is therefore linked with the theme of human limitations and is part of Paul's rite of passage that follows the loss of his dreams. But the adult Paul is still moved by the beauty of the natural world at the novel's close, suggesting that his emotional position is much healthier than Keller's. Indeed he is inclined to attribute inner beauty to the man whose experience taught him to be wary of its external manifestations. (See 'Different interpretations' below for more on the idea of beauty.)

Ethnic and racial diversity

This theme is developed through both Keller's experience of anti-Semitism in 1930s Europe, and the multicultural nature of Darwin as Paul experiences it in the 1960s.

Goldsworthy subtly draws attention to Australia's shameful past and contemporary racism with two parallel events in the narrative. As the Crabbe family travel through the desert on their way from Darwin to Adelaide for their Christmas holiday, Paul remembers a vision of an Aboriginal man. The tribesman is one of the powerfully evocative 'odd dream images' Paul recalls from that period:

> a taxi heading south into that same desert, pulling over at some arranged spot and disgorging its passenger – a bearded black tribesman who paid his fare and strode off into the hot dunes, barefoot, carrying nothing but spears. (p.53)

This is a positive image of the tribesman who combines a practical aspect of civilisation (the taxi) with his traditional culture (the spears). He also strides purposefully, implying that he knows exactly where he is going. But like the other 'dream images' Paul recalls (the sky made black by budgerigars, and a tiny square of lawn under a sprinkler in the middle of the desert), this vision is strange and unusual to him.

Another event involving a car, a trip to Adelaide and a part-Aboriginal male provides an echo of this memory. When *Rough Stuff* travels to Adelaide, Reggie, the Chinese-Aboriginal drummer, is absent, his place in the van taken by Rick Whitely. As Paul asks, 'why would a middle-aged disc jockey want to play drums with a band of school kids'? (p.105). Because of Whitely's presence (or influence) the boys have voted to leave Reggie behind, and Scotty's sense of guilt and Paul's incredulity underline this implicitly racist act (p.108).

DIFFERENT INTERPRETATIONS

Different interpretations arise from different responses to a text. However, while there is no single correct reading or interpretation of a text, an interpretation is more than an 'opinion' – it is the justification of a point of view on the text as a whole, or on one element of it. To present an interpretation of the text based on your point of view you must use a logical argument and relevant evidence from the text to support and strengthen it.

Different views of Keller

The enigmatic character of Eduard Keller is open to a range of interpretations which in turn influence how we understand the novel as a whole. Is *Maestro* the story of a wonderful teacher whose student simply cannot rise to the challenges presented to him? Or is it rather the story of a gifted musician who is now so embittered about the past that he is unable to convey the emotional rewards of playing music? Does Keller's insight enable Paul to develop his potential? Or do his relentless criticisms actually prevent Paul from becoming a concert pianist?

There are no 'right' and 'wrong' answers to these questions. However, they do suggest fairly extreme positions. The most plausible interpretations would acknowledge Keller's complexities and the terrible events he has experienced, and point out his virtues as well as his flaws.

An important quotation to consider is Paul's remark that Keller was 'the worst possible teacher' (p.148). Taking this at face value leads to a simplistic view of Keller – one that greatly exaggerates his faults. The initial qualification is significant: 'In this sense', that is, in the sense of teaching Paul 'self-criticism'. In many other senses, as Paul acknowledges, his experiences as a student of Keller were invaluable.

Different views of Paul

Since Paul is the narrator, any interpretation needs to carefully distinguish *Paul's* view of himself from *our* view of him as readers. The older, mature Paul who looks back on his younger self is often critical, and the teenaged Paul does make some poor choices – notably his betrayals of Bennie and Rosie. But does he over-emphasise his flaws? While Paul often draws our attention to his own arrogance and smugness (pp.70, 123), he is never so self-satisfied that he stops trying to improve, and he also displays many positive qualities. For example, he ensures that his arrangements for the band allow for 'all the members of the band [to] participate' (p.86); he is disappointed when Reggie is left behind in Darwin; he regrets his betrayals of Bennie and Rosie, which are never repeated.

Is Paul, in the end, a failure as a musician? Although he expresses his deep disappointment and frustration, he is actually a very successful, prize-winning pianist, and to gain an academic position in his mid-twenties shows a high level of achievement and recognition by his professional peers. As with Keller, a range of different views of Paul's character are possible. Whichever overall view you take, remember to take into account his positive qualities as well as his negative ones.

Different views of beauty

The novel offers a number of perspectives on the concept of beauty, and how important it is in life. It is interesting to consider whether the novel endorses one view more than another.

For Paul, beauty is something that sweeps you away through intense emotional responses and experiences – as he hears Keller play the *Liebestod* Paul is 'transported again to that same sensual, aching zone', and he thinks it the 'most beautiful music' he has ever heard (p.74). Paul sees beauty as inseparable from music, and as closely linked to powerful emotions, especially those of love.

On the other hand, Keller appears very sceptical of beauty: 'Never trust the beautiful ... Beauty simplifies', he warns Paul (p.50). For Keller, music should not be confused with emotion, but is something more abstract and impersonal: 'a kind of arithmetic' (p.50). One way of reading this is as a reflection of Keller's traumatic past, the terrible events that have led Keller to distrust emotional responses and, therefore, any music that relies on them. Keller's rejection of beauty also extends to the city of Vienna, the surface beauty of which hides 'the hypocrisy within' (p.45).

However, another reading could see Keller as simply appreciating a different kind of beauty, one which depends less on the emotions or superficial appearances, and more on a deeper understanding of structure and form. He values things that are 'infinitely complex. Full of nuance. Rich beyond any reduction' (p.50). This more abstract kind of beauty is not immediately obvious to Paul, for whom 'the world of the senses' is dominant over the 'world of the mind' (p.75). Keller's experience and maturity, though, enable him to value music, and perceive beauty, in a different yet equally valid way.

QUESTIONS & ANSWERS

Essay topics

The essay topics below show a range of possible styles and formats, and are suitable for senior English assessment tasks and examinations.

1. 'Because Paul's and Keller's stories are so intertwined, the painful relationship between them becomes the focus of the novel.' Discuss.
2. 'Paul maintains his ambivalent attitude towards Keller throughout the novel.' Discuss.
3. 'In *Maestro*, neither Paul nor Keller are wholly admirable characters.' Do you agree?
4. 'Vienna and Darwin, worlds apart in musical taste and history, are both vitally relevant to our understanding of Paul and Keller.' Discuss.
5. "And thus, while I listened the future became the present, unchallenged; and all too soon the regretted past."
   Discuss the role of the past in *Maestro*.

6. 'Paul's rite of passage from childhood through adolescence to maturity is dominated by the influence of Eduard Keller.' Discuss.
7. 'As he tells his own story, Paul reveals himself to be a sensitive, intelligent and likable character well aware of his youthful weaknesses.' Do you agree?
8. 'Humour and human warmth to some extent compensate for the evil and pain in the novel, but in the end, suffering dominates Paul's and Keller's lives.' Discuss.
9. 'The first-person narrative tells us much about Paul, but little about Keller.' Do you agree?
10. How does *Maestro* convey the unique challenges and rewards of childhood?

Analysing a sample topic

'The first-person narrative tells us much about Paul, but little about Keller.' Do you agree?

This topic focuses on the use of narrative point of view in the novel. It is important to keep your own focus on this technique, and not let your answer become simply a description or profile of the two characters. Think about *how* the narrative voice tells us about the two characters, and *how* it reveals or conceals information about them.

Because this topic has the familiar form of a contention (statement about the text) followed by a prompt ('Discuss' or 'Do you agree?'), you can agree, disagree or partially agree/disagree. Remember that your assessors do not expect you to completely agree with the contention. Indeed, more interesting and complex responses can result when you think about ways in which the statement is *not* true.

The following points could be used to agree with the contention:

- The first-person narrative describes everything from Paul's point of view; other characters' perspectives and feelings are only presented through direct speech.

- Paul's experiences, thoughts, feelings, hopes and fears are presented in detail.
- Keller's inner thoughts, feelings and memories are concealed because he is very reluctant to talk about them – so they remain largely mysterious to the reader.

On the other hand, the following points could be used to place pressure on the contention:

- Paul only reveals what he wants us to know, and the first-person narrative means that a more balanced, external perspective of his character is unavailable – we lack, for instance, a detailed description of his physical appearance (such as we receive for Keller).
- We do not see Paul as others see him – Rosie's view of Paul, for example, is not presented. The first-person account tells us much about Paul, but only from *Paul's* perspective, and in this way can be seen as quite limited.
- We learn a great deal about Keller from his conversations and interactions with others – not just Paul, but also John and Nancy Crabbe (e.g. pp.43–6), and Paul's grandmother (pp.101–3). We also have Henisch's account of Keller in the 1930s, adding an extra layer to our understanding.

Overall, you should decide which of these points you are most convinced by and decide on your central argument. A partial agreement/disagreement might be the most useful approach here: we do learn a lot about Paul, but the narrative also allows us to learn much about Keller. This argument would allow most of the above points to be used, giving considerable range and complexity to the response.

SAMPLE ANSWER

'Paul's rite of passage from childhood through adolescence to maturity is dominated by the influence of Eduard Keller.' Discuss.

Paul's rite of passage from childhood through adolescence to maturity is closely interwoven with the life of Eduard Keller, his elderly and reticent Viennese piano teacher. The adult Paul, who narrates *Maestro* retrospectively, attributes great significance to the years he spent in Darwin, not just because of Keller's major influence and Paul's musical successes and disappointments, but also because this was the time when he met Rosie, the girl who would later become his wife. Nevertheless, Keller's influence remains strong even years later when Paul is in Europe unsuccessfully seeking musical fame. He identifies strongly with Keller's loneliness at this time. The mature Paul is finally forced to face his musical and personal limitations when he is called back to Darwin as the maestro is dying and we see how crucial Keller has been in shaping Paul's life.

There are, of course, other significant influences on the adolescent Paul. As a lonely, serious fifteen-year-old in a new city Paul is victimised by bullies at his new school, an experience that reinforces his isolation from his peers. He is very close to his parents, both as their only child and because he shares their love of music. He is humiliated by the demandingly exact Keller but intrigued by his mysterious background. Keller can be thought of as the sustained note in Paul's life that is filled with the music of his parents. To compensate for his shyness and isolation, Paul adopts a tough veneer. He is known at school as 'Big Mouth' and is arrogant with the maestro. Like the maestro, who has cultivated a gruffly polite facade, Paul is uncomfortable with who he is.

The delight of his proud parents when Paul achieves an excellent result in his Associate examination encourages him in his resolve to become a professional pianist. However, when the maestro comes to dinner with the family he is critical of Paul's performance, perhaps compensating for his affection for Paul which is shown by his acceptance of the dinner invitation, or perhaps regretting the fragmentary revelations he has made about his past during the reign of Hitler's Third Reich. Paul is humiliated by Keller's observation that he is 'self-satisfied' and by Keller's assertion that, although Paul's playing is technically flawless, it lacks a vital element, the 'little bits' which distinguish a good pianist from a great one. Keller's criticism, however, only fires Paul's resolve to overcome his deficiencies.

The older Paul recognises Keller's contradictory influence on his music. During the Wet, Keller's musical tastes narrow to the point where Paul is only practising scales and any emotionally expressive music is forbidden. At other times the maestro shows Paul perfection in his own playing and allows some emotional expression in music, but then teaches him to play in a too narrowly disciplined way. In this way, Keller's influence can be seen to be restrictive as well as powerful.

Paul's frustration with the discipline of classical music is somewhat compensated for in his relationship with Rosie and his participation in *Rough Stuff*. Rather than achieving an idealised classical plateau, he expresses his emotions through sex and the driving rhythms of rock music. Paul achieves moderate fame with the band and, importantly, is accepted by the boys who once bullied him. But he still lacks a strong sense of identity, reflected in the ease with which he is swayed by others. He betrays Bennie, his alter-ego, to Jimmy Papas; and Rosie with the beautiful but shallow school goddess, Megan. Paul's recognition of the squalor of his fame, and the preciousness of his relationship with Rosie, mark further stages in his rite of passage. It is Keller who steps in and suggests he enter the Conservatorium piano competition, recognising that Paul is in danger of being distracted by the superficiality of popular music.

With the disappointment of his third placing in the competition and Keller's assertion that Paul will not learn any more in Europe than Keller can teach him in Darwin, Paul's dreams of fame become shaky. However, he cannot give up his desire to be world famous. When he is in Europe he experiences a sense of exile and failure and identifies strongly with the maestro, who has chosen to exile himself on the other side of the world. In Europe, Paul learns that the disciplinarian who distrusts beauty and Romantic music had previously been a pianist who loved big sounds and had recorded Wagner's *Liebestod*. Because the operas of the anti-Semitic Wagner were used as propaganda by Hitler, and because his wife was a Wagner specialist, the maestro distrusts emotional expression to the point of obsession. The mature Paul now understands the debate between head and heart, emotion and reason that the tormented maestro fought internally. Understanding finally helps to release him from the maestro's dominating influence.

After Keller dies, it is clear that Paul has a full understanding of the maestro's ambivalent influence on his music and life, yet he refers to Keller as a great man. Throughout *Maestro* the mature narrator shows some contempt for the sensual boy he was and the foolish dreams he had. But at the end of the novel Paul places Keller's influence into a broader perspective, allowing him to see the importance of balance in his life.

Goldsworthy suggests that we must have dreams to help give meaning and purpose to our lives. Paul may be intensely dissatisfied with his teaching position but his family provides him with essential love and support. Like his father, Paul knows he needs a balance between emotion and reason, and the last phase of his journey towards maturity is reached in his nostalgic but complete acceptance of his rite of passage. This acceptance is also of Keller's dominant role during his teenage years – an influence that powerfully shapes the adult Paul, but that he eventually must balance with the lessons that life itself has taught him.

REFERENCES & READING

Text

Goldsworthy, Peter 1996, *Maestro*, HarperCollins, Sydney.

References

Burbidge, P. and Sutton, R. 1979, eds., *The Wagner Companion*, Faber & Faber, London.

Carr, William 1978, *Hitler: A Study in Personality and Politics*, Edward Arnold, London.

Kershaw, Ian 1991, *Hitler*, Longman, London.

Kershaw, Ian 1987, *The Hitler Myth*, Oxford UP, Oxford.

Murphy, Brian 1982, *Dictionary of Australian History*, Fontana, Sydney.

Osborne, Charles 1977, *Wagner and his World*, Thames and Hudson, London.

Longyear, Rey M. 1969, *Nineteenth Century Romanticism in Music*, Prentice-Hall, Englewood Cliffs, New Jersey.

Website

Peter Goldsworthy's website, www.petergoldsworthy.com